Easton: City of Resources

Easton, Pennsylvania, at the Height of the Industrial Revolution

Bruce Fackenthal

©2021 by Bruce Fackenthal

All rights reserved. No part of this publication may be reproduced
or transmitted in any form or by any means, electronic or mechanical,
including photocopying, recording, or any other information storage
and retrieval system, without the written permission of the publisher.

Internet addresses given in this book were accurate at the time it went to press.

Printed in the United States of America
Published in Hellertown, PA
Cover and interior design and illustrations by Bruce Fackenthal

Library of Congress Control Number: 2021914830
ISBN Number: 978-1-952481-48-2 soft cover

For more information or to place bulk orders, contact the publisher at
Jennifer@BrightCommunications.net or author at bruce@fackenthal.com.

BrightCommunications.net

Easton, Pennsylvania

Introduction

By the late 19th century Easton, Pennsylvania, had evoloutioned from a pre-Revoloutionary British frontier village into a prosperous American industrial city. Easton became a manufacturing and distrubution center for the surrounding area. As early as the 1820's, the Bushkill Creek, with over fifty mills between Easton and Tatamy, was considered to be the most industrialized "river" in America. With the creation of the Lehigh, Delaware, and Morris canals, Easton was positioned early for prime distribution to New York and Philadelphia. When the railroads became the primary mode of transportation, Easton was prepared, established with years of trade, and was also able to utilize new trade routes provided by the railroads. This book focuses on Easton in the late nineteenth century and the early twentieth century, when America was at the peak of the Industrial Revolution, and Easton flourished with economic prosperity.

The Philadelphia & Easton Trolley Line

Excursions to Easton were offered by the Philadelphia and Easton trolley line. The four-hour trip from Philadelphia to Easton cost eighty cents. Passengers from Philadelphia could pick up the Willow Grove car at Eighth and Walnut Streets. At the Willow Grove Station, travelers would transfer to the Doylestown trolley that would take passengers from Doylestown over to the scenic Delaware River, then arriving at the Lehigh Valley Railroad Station in Easton. Once in Easton, travelers could ask for a pass to the College Hill Line. At Center Square, incoming guests would transfer to a line that brought them to the Shawnee Spring Station. From Shawnee Spring, passengers would get on the Weygadt Mountian Railroad and then travel up the mountian and on to Easton's premier resort, Paxinosa Inn.

Phila. & Easton Trolley on way to Paxinosa Inn, on the summit of Weygadt Mountain, near Easton PA

The Weygadt Mountain Railroad

The Weygadt Mountain Railroad was an electric railway that was completed in 1893 to give greater access to Paxinosa Inn and the surrounding scenery. Prior to the trolley, a stagecoach was the only means of transportation to the inn. The two-mile line went from Shawnee Spring to the eastern edge of Weygadt Mountain overlooking the Delaware River, where it turned westward along the top of the ridge and headed toward the inn. Easton was the third city in the United States to get an electric trolley system after Baltimore, Maryland, and Reading, Pennsylvania.

Rounding Weygadt Mountain to Paxinosa

Paxinosa Inn 1888 to 1905

Opened on July 3, 1888, Paxinosa Inn was Easton's elegant resort at the summit of Weygadt Mountain. The inn was named after the Shawnee Chief Paxinosa who supported the English during the French and Indian War. Paxinosa Inn catered to wealthy Philadelphians and New Yorkers looking to escape the cities in the summer months. The inn was also known as a popular spot where Lafayette College students held dances and class reunions. On the morning of July 11, 1905, a fire started by an overheated flue in the laundry. The fire spread so quickly that an hour later the building was in ruins. In 1908, the inn was rebuilt in brick and considered fireproof. By 1931, the Great Depression had taken its toll on business, and Paxinosa Inn suspiciously burned to the ground for a second time.

THIS popular resort overlooking the Delaware and Lehigh Valleys, will be opened in June for the season of 1893, under the proprietorship of W. A. ELMORE, late of the Fifth Avenue Hotel, New York City.

Paxinosa Inn rests on the crest of Weygat Mountain, two miles north of Easton, Pennsylvania, is 1,000 feet above the sea, and 600 feet above the Delaware River, which is immediately below the inn. It is heated by steam, lighted by gas and electricity, is handsomly appointed, has unsurpassed views, and accommodates 300 guests, every one of which has an unobstructed rural view extending for miles. Two hours from New York by Lehigh Valley or New Jersey Central Railroads. Two hours from Philadelphia by Pennsylvania, or Philadelphia and Reading. Electric road formerly running to Shawnee Spring, now being built to the Inn, will transport passengers and baggage from depots.

Bowling, Boating, Fishing, Tennis, Billiards, Music, and Dancing Hall.
EVERYTHING STRICTLY FIRST-CLASS.
W.A. ELMORE, Fifth Avenue Hotel, New York City, or EASTON, PENNSYLVANIA

OVERLOOKING EASTON AND PHILLIPSBURG

ON THE LAWN – PAXINOSA INN
ON WEYGADT MOUNTAIN, NEAR EASTON, PA.

THE TROLLEY STATION AND TENNIS COURTS

THE HIKING TRAILS

WALK TO PAVILION PAXINOSA INN
ON WEYGADT MOUNTAIN, NEAR EASTON, PA.

THE PAVILION AT PAXINOSA INN
ON WEYGADT MOUNTAIN, NEAR EASTON PA.

THE PAVILION

8

THE SUMMIT KNOWN AS SAINT ANTHONY'S NOSE

THE CLIFFS AT PAXINOSA INN ON WEYGADT MOUNTAIN, NEAR EASTON, PA.

On the Cliffs at Weygadt Mountain

The Second Paxinosa Inn 1908-1931

The Second Paxinosa Inn 1908-1931

Crossing Tatamy Road en Route to Bushkill Park

The Easton and Nazareth Rail Company built Bushkill Park as a trolley destination. The park was owned by the Easton and Nazareth Rail Company, and it was leased and operated by the Hay Trolley Line, owned by the Easton Transit Company.

Over the Bridge to the Entrance of Bushkill Park

THE STONE BRIDGE AT BUSHKILL PARK

BOATING ON THE BUSHKILL

Bushkill Park was opened in 1902. The park once featured a pagoda that originally was used as a concession stand. Later a spiral sliding board was added to the exterior of the structure. Early Bushkill Park also offered swimming, roller skating, boating, picnic groves, box ball alleys, a dance hall, and the Comus Theater, where silent films were often featured. Thomas Long leased Bushkill Park in 1933. He and his father had purchased and installed a hand-carved carousel that had originally been used at Island Park. Later attractions featured a games arcade, a shooting gallery, a funhouse, and several mechanical rides, such as the Comet roller coaster, the Whip, bumper cars, a miniture railroad, a dark ride named the Pretzel, Salt and Pepper shaker, and the Merry Mixer.

The Comus Theater at Bushkill Park

The Walking Bridge

The Picnic Grove

The Dam at Bushkill Park

The Boat Dock at Bushkill Park

18

Bushkill Park Roller Rink

The Dance Pavillion

The Arcade

CROSSING THE TRESTLE AT CHAIN DAM, HEADING TO ISLAND PARK

The Easton Transit Company created Island Park at Smith Island on the Lehigh River as a way to increase weekend fares. The ten-cent fare included admission and a round trip from Easton and back. The park opened in July 1894 to a crowd of 3,000 people. Island Park was an amusement park that offered a Ferris wheel, horseback riding, a merry-go-round, boating, a roller coaster, live music, theater, silent films, and a dance hall. In 1917, an ice jam on the Lehigh River destroyed the trolley trestle. After the Easton Transit Company repaired the trestle, another ice jam in 1919 destroyed it again. Island Park's last season was 1919.

Entrance to Island Park

BOATING ON THE LEHIGH RIVER AT ISLAND PARK

The Dancing Pavilion

The Casino Theater

The Island Park Roller Coaster

The Midway

The Bandshell

The Miniature Railroad at Island Park

THE SAND PIT   THE FERRIS WHEEL

THE PAVILIONS

The Merry-Go-Round

The Boat Landing

THE
UNITED STATES
HOTEL

GEORGE H. VINCENT, PROPRIETOR.

The Largest and Best Appointed Hotel in Easton

OMNIBUSES AND CABS AT HOTEL TO MEET TRAINS AT DEPOTS.

LOCATION---THIRD and SPRING GARDEN STREETS,

EASTON, PENNA.

Looking West on Spring Garden Street at the United States Hotel

THE KARLDON HOTEL AT THE NORTHWEST CORNER OF THIRD AND SPRING GARDEN

In the 1700s, the property at the northwest corner of Third and Spring Garden Streets had a colonial era, limestone hotel that was named the Rising Sun Hotel. The Rising Sun Hotel was known to cater largely to the men who worked on the rivers. Later, the name was changed to the Black Horse Hotel, which was demolished in 1853. That same year the United States Hotel was built there. The hotel was purchased in 1908 by William Kuebler of the Kuebler Brewing family, who renamed the hotel the Karldon Hotel after his sons Karl and Donald. Donald Kuebler was murdered there by Alexander A. Lorings on May 26, 1923, at the age of 21.

The Karldon Dining Room

The Karldon Lobby

The Hotel Huntington

Built in 1903

The Hotel Huntington Lobby

The Hotel Huntington Dining Room

The Hotel Huntington Diner

Hotel Easton Lounge and Dining Hall

The Seitz Brewing Company on Bushkill Street

Seitz Brewery started as the Seitz and Goundie brewery in 1821 in a wheat field near Second and Ferry Streets. The partnership dissolved in 1823, and Fredrick Seitz continued with the brewery. At the time, the brewery employed six people and annually produced 500 barrels of beer. In 1851, Seitz invented and patented an improved method of preparing corn for brewing and distilling. This method reduced the amount of malt required to produce the sugar in the brewing process. Deliveries were done with four horse-drawn wagons that serviced a 25-mile radius. Each wagon carried five tons of beer.

Fredrick Seitz

In 1855, Seitz began utilizing canal boat delivery. Each canal boat carried 80 tons of beer, and the brewery's distribution expanded to Mauch Chunk, Pennsylvania, on the Lehigh Canal and to New York City via the Morris Canal. By 1898, the company built a new brewery next to their bottling house on Bushkill Street. The new brewery produced 50,000 barrels of beer annually. In 1904, the last remaining family member, John Seitz, sold the buisness to the brewmaster and partnered with Easton businessmen, who increased production to 65,000 barrels a year. During Prohibition, the brewery sold a soft drink called Seitz. The brewery had come under control

of the infamous "Beer Baron," Max Hassel. Seitz Brewery had been caught selling high-powered beer despite Prohibition. They lost their license after being identified as part of a brewery syndicate controlled by Max Hassel. A rubber hose was set up under the Delaware River where beer was pumped to the American Horseshoe factory in Phillipsburg, New Jersey. The brewery reopened as the Osterstock Brewing Co. in February 1935. In 1938, the brewery was shut down for creating counterfeit bottle caps. Bottle caps had been used as a method of taxation identification. The result of getting caught using the counterfeit caps was bankruptcy, and the end of a 117-year-old business.

Kuebler Brewery started as the partnership of Willibald Kuebler and Charles Glantz. For the first few years, they brewed small quantities of beer at the corner of Church and Bank Streets. In 1852, they built a brewery along the Delaware Canal. This location offered a limestone cave that had been dug out and turned into a series of vaults to store beer. The location was at the confluence of the Lehigh and Delaware Canals, giving acess to distribution. From 1870 to 1879, Glantz and Kuebler also had a brewery 35 miles northwest in the town of Mauch Chunk. In 1878, Mr. Kuebler

became the sole proprietor of the Easton Brewery. 1894 was a productive year for Kuebler Brewery. Mr. Kuebler created and marketed a product designed for washing and filtering brewers' shavings, chips, and cellulose. It was claimed that the process turned the work of eight men into the work of two, while using less water. That same year, Kuebler built a bottling house, put together a refrigerating plant, created a store room, and built stables, giving the brewery the ability to produce 200 barrels of beer a day. In 1898, Willibald passed away, and his three sons, William, Charles, and Frank, began conducting business as Willibald Kuebler's Sons.

Other brewers of Easton have included Bushkill, Marbacher, Take and Veile, J. Cummings, Andrew Newman, Markley, J.Steel, GA Kohl, Kohl and Bean, S. Everhart, W. Everhart, and Jacob Schneider.

Photos courtesy of Northampton County Historical and Genealogical Society

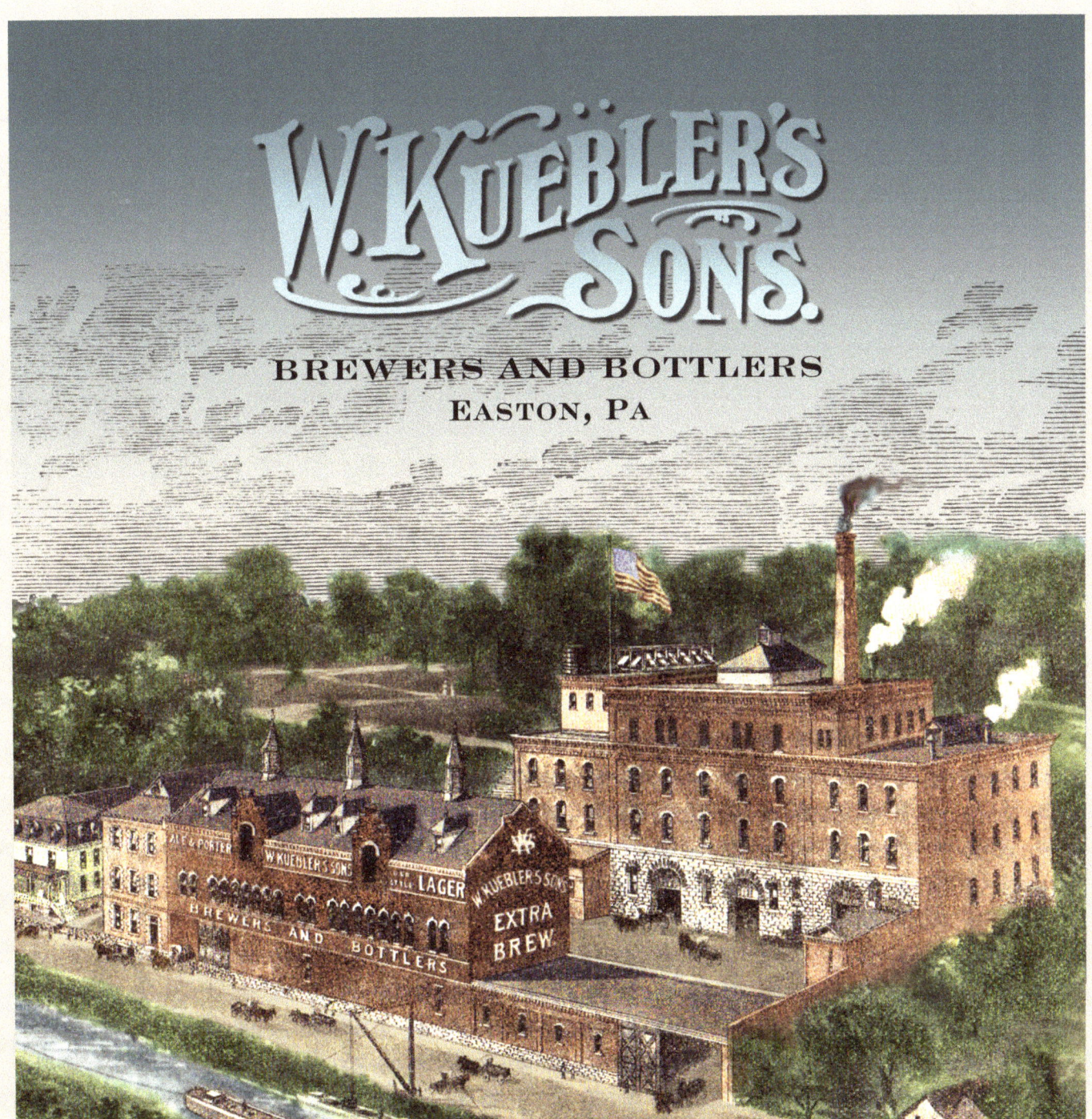

LAWRENCE ORGAN WORKS!

LIMITED.

Factory, Office and Wareroom:

320 and 322 South Tenth Street, and 939 Walnut Street, Easton, Penna.

DO YOU KNOW THAT THE
LEAR PIANO–STYLE ORGAN

Was the first **SEVEN-OCTAVE ORGAN** widely introduced, and has probably a larger scale than all other **SEVEN–OCTAVES** combined! **THAT** recent invention, consisting of the patented **LEAR** Nickel Pedal Arrangement (which makes pumping easy), the Patented **LEAR** Coupler Arrangement (the only contrivance to put couplers on any set of reeds **WITHOUT DISTURBING HANDS OR FEET**, and the Patented **LEAR** Key–Leveller (which keeps the line of keys even and straight) are the Most Valuable Improvements made in Reed–organ construction in the past few years; and that they place the **LEAR** still further beyond competition and make it the Only One of a kind.

DO YOU KNOW also that the **LEAR** is rapidly supplanting, and is a marvelous improvement over the old–style common Parlor Organ, for it plays piano and organ music, has seven octaves of keys, looks exactly like a handsome Upright Piano, and costs only one-third as much.

H. LEHR & CO., Mfrs., EASTON, PA.

WM. H. KELLER

LARGEST STOCK!   LOWEST PRICES!   EASIEST TERMS!

Pianos and Organs FOR RENT, and Part Rent Allowed if Purchased.

TUNING AND REPAIRING!

Nos. 219 & 221 Northampton Street, Easton, Penna.

C. M. Hapgood Shoe Co.

Manufacturers & Dealers in

Sales Agents for Easton Boot & Shoe Co.

Boots, Shoes & Rubbers.

Every pair will be Solid Sole-Leather Counters and Warranted in Every Respect.

Buy no other make until you see these Boots and get our prices, which will be as low as the lowest.

Address all orders to

C. M. HAPGOOD, PRESIDENT OF THE EASTON BOOT AND SHOE CO.
EASTON, PA.

The Residence of C. M. Hapgood at 14th and Northampton Streets

The Frank Wilson Residence at North Delaware Drive

Herman Simon was a German immigrant who started his career as a silk buyer in New York City. Mr. Simon and his brother Robert built the R & H Simon Silk Mill in Easton in 1883, expanding their business from Union Hill, New Jersey. The Easton location offered water power, a young labor force, and an established distribution network. At one time, the Simon Mill was the largest producer of black silk ribbon in the world. Robert Simon passed away in 1901, leaving Herman to run the company. The following year, Mr. Simon built a mansion on North Third Street in Easton to provide his wife and daughter access to downtown and to offer a place to entertain guests.

The Simon Residence at 13th and Bushkill Streets

Herman Simon

The Herman Simon Mansion on North Third Street

Built in 1902

R. & H. SIMON
FACTORIES

Easton, Pa., Union Hill, N. J., Paterson, N. J.

The Chipman Residence on North Delaware Drive

TREADWELL ENGINEERING COMPANY ON WILLIAM PENN HIGHWAY

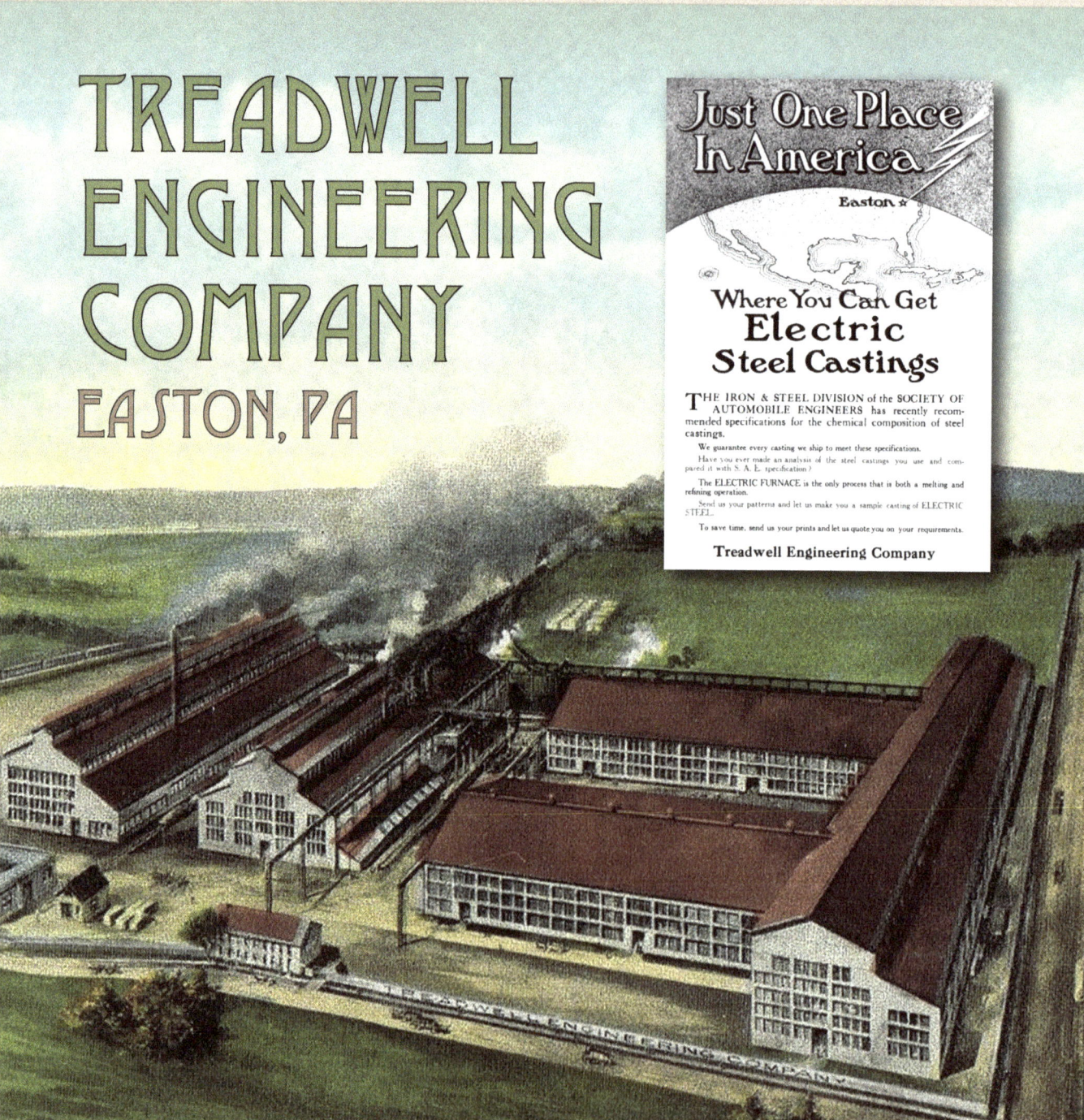

The Mack Printing Company on Northampton Street

Howard Rinek was the president of the Rinek Cordage Company on Bushkill Drive. In addition to successfully managing his family's rope-manufacturing business, Mr. Rinek proved to be a progressive visionary. The Rinek home was the first residence in Easton to have incandescent lighting. A two-horsepower engine powered a dynamo that turned at 1,400 rpm. This self-generating power plant produced enough electricity to power the 60 lights throughout the home. The success of Rinek's powerplant led to him organizing and managing the Edison Illuminating Company of Easton. In the early days of electricity, the demand for lighting and power exceeded the capacity of the plant, especially during evenings when light was needed more. Mr. Rinek focused on providing power for electric street railways, and he set his sights on upgrading a trolley service that went from the base of College Hill to the top of Chestnut Street. The existing rail line was a double-wired 220 volt system and did not work well. Mr. Rinek secured a contract that provided a single-line system that delivered 500 volts. This was an early step in establishing multiple trolley lines in Easton and Phillipsburg, New Jersey. Mr. Rinek's son, Charles Norvin Rinek, became a model railroad enthusiast and had a miniture railroad installed around the grounds of the family's College Hill estate.

The Howard Rinek Residence on Paxinosa Street

The Kepler Mill

Binney and Smith

Edwin Binney   C. Harold Smith

Edwin Binney and cousin, C. Harold Smith, began the partnership of Binney & Smith in Peekskill, NY, in 1885. Early products included red oxide pigments for painting red barns and carbon black for car tires. In 1900, the company purchased the former Kepler mill in Easton, PA, and began producing slate school pencils. Two years later, Binney & Smith made the first dustless school chalk. It was so successful it won a gold medal at the 1902 St. Louis World Exposition. In the following year, Binney & Smith made the first box of eight Crayola crayons. The box sold for a nickel and contained black, brown, blue, red, violet, orange, yellow, and green. The Crayola name was coined by Alice Binney, wife of company founder Edwin and a former school teacher. It came from "craie," the French word for "chalk," and "ola," for "oleaginous," or "oily." Today the Crayola brand is known throughout the world.

* Photos courtesy of Crayola

The Binney and Smith Company along the Bushkill Creek

Photo-Panovec/Fackenthal

WHAT IS A DIXIE?

A danty, inviting individual container for good things to eat and drink. In addition to Dixies for ice cream, Individual Dixies for drinks are found in the stations and coaches of railroads, in offices, theaters, hotels, restaurants, and better soda fountains. And at most drug, stationary, and department stores, you can get Dixies in convenient cartons for home or picnic use.

5¢ Ice Cream DIXIES

Whenever and wherever you get a 5¢ Ice Cream Dixie, you can always be sure of finding it filled with high-standard ice cream! The Dixie franchise is granted exclusively to manufacturers of high standard ice cream. In that sense, the Dixie Franchise is your protection. And the Dixie Blue Scroll Design, which identifies the original and only genuine Dixie, becomes your guarantee of delicious, healthful, and clean ice cream standard.

INDIVIDUAL DRINKING CUP CO., INC., EASTON, PA
Original Makers of the Paper Cup

The Dixie Cup Factory

Lawrence Luellen of Boston conceived of a one-piece pleated cup constructed of folded paper in 1907. The paper would be treated with paraffin to hold the folds in place. The cups would be stacked in the "Luellen Cup & Water Vendor," and for one penny, the consumer would have an individual sanitary cup of cold water dispensed. In 1908, Luellen added and patented a "frusto-conical" form with a separate bottom piece. In the same year, Luellen gathered a group of investors and incorporated the American Water Supply Company of New England. With the assistance of inventor and engineer Eugene H. Taylor, Luellen established the mechanisms necessary to manufacture paper cups.

In 1909, distribution was expanded with the creation of the American Water Supply Companies of New York and New Jersey. Secretary and treasurer Hugh Moore became the director, and along with Luellen formed the Public Cup Vendor Company. This company focused on vending leases and cup sales. In 1910, the American Water Supply Companies of New England, New York, and New Jersey, and the Public Cup Vendor Company were consolidated into the Individual Drinking Cup Company of New York, with Moore as president.

The demand for paper cups increased during the flu epidemic following World War I. What was named as the Health Kup in 1912 would be renamed the Dixie Cup in 1919. After 10 years in New York City, the company needed to expand. Moore chose to build a new 80,000 square foot factory in Easton. The new plant opened in 1921 with 78 employees, 28 employees who moved from New York, and 50 new hires from Easton.

After moving to Easton, the company found success in packaging individual servings of ice cream. Ice Cream Dixies became an instant hit with the help of "The Dixie Circus," a radio program that aired nationally and brought the Dixie brand into the American consciousness.

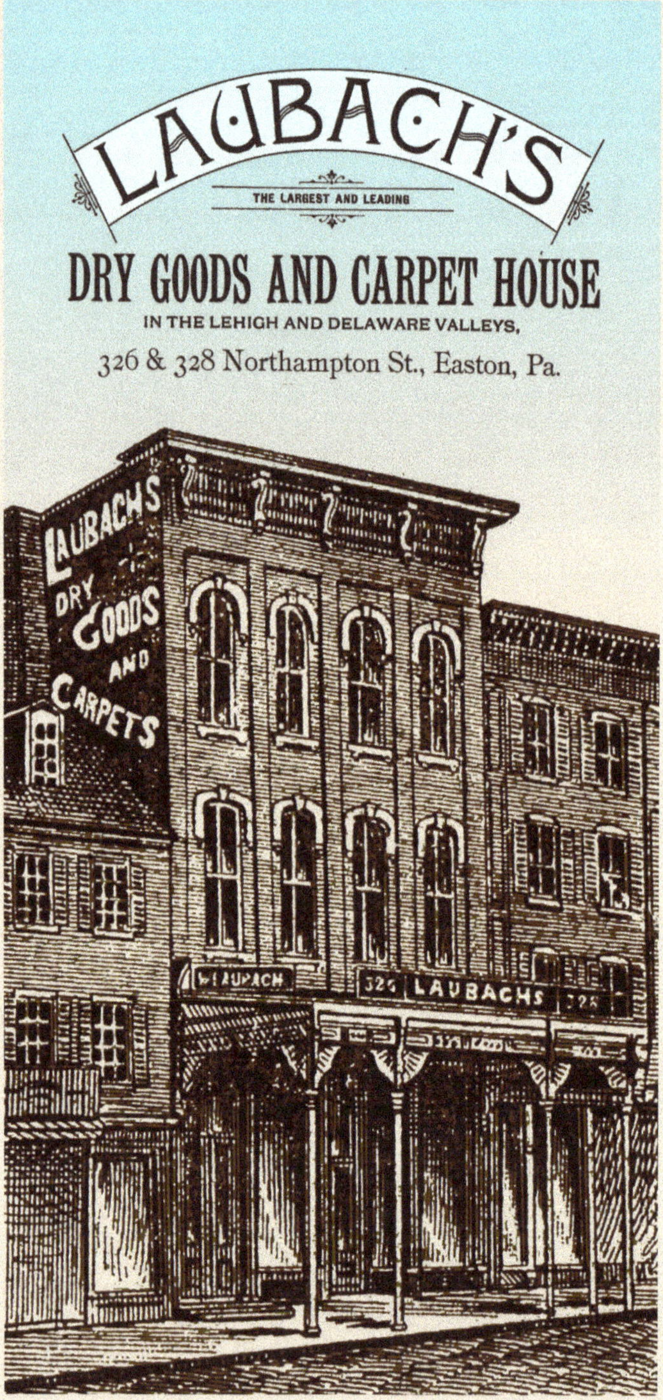
LAUBACH'S
THE LARGEST AND LEADING
DRY GOODS AND CARPET HOUSE
IN THE LEHIGH AND DELAWARE VALLEYS,
326 & 328 Northampton St., Easton, Pa.
LAUBACH'S
DRY
GOODS
AND
CARPETS
LAUBACHS

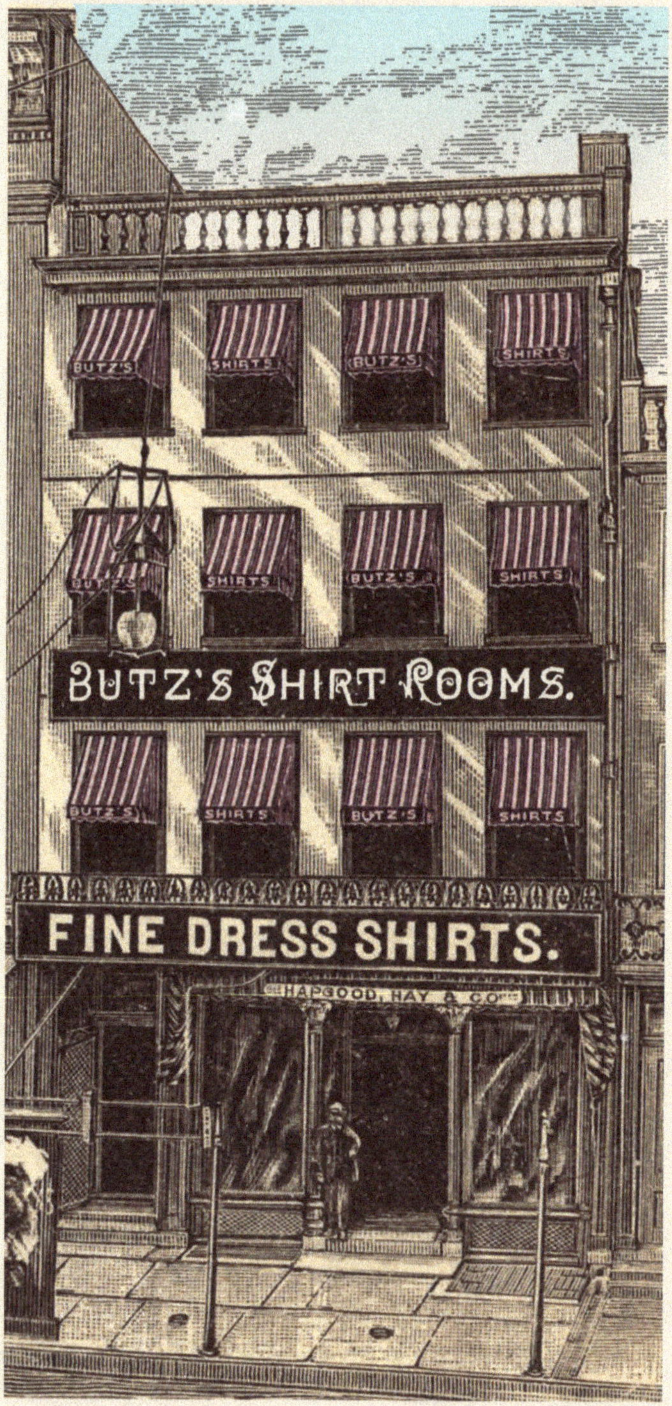
BUTZ'S SHIRT ROOMS.
FINE DRESS SHIRTS.

FIRST NATIONAL BANK
—OF—
EASTON

EDWARD F. STEWART, PRESIDENT.

JOHN F. GWINNER, CASHIER.

CAPITAL, $400,000.00.

SURPLUS —AND— Undivided Profits, $120,000.

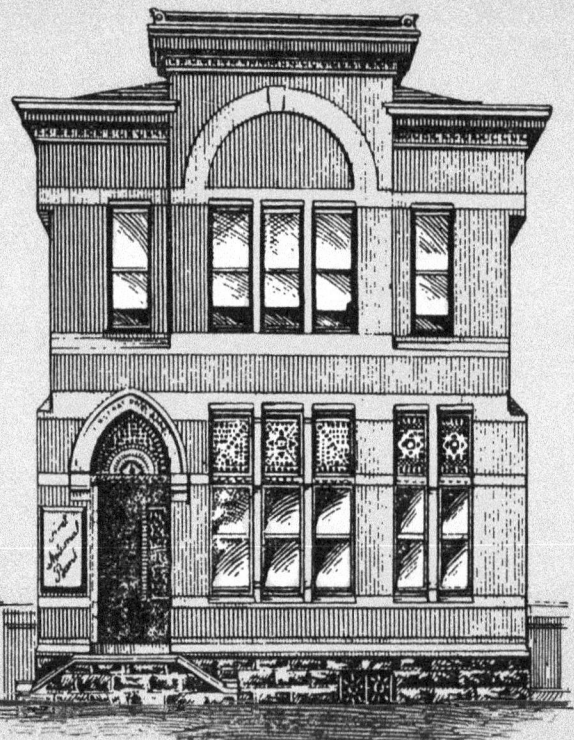

A BANK OF DISCOUNT AND DEPOSIT.

The Easton Trust Company

Northampton National Bank at Fourth and Northampton Streets

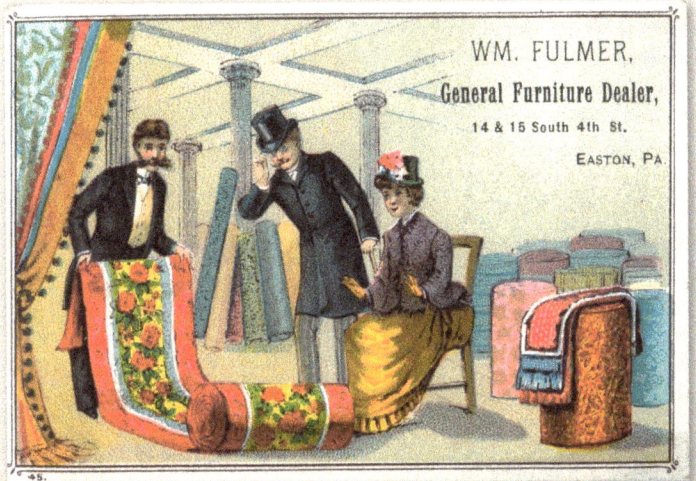

The Drake Building at the Corner of Third and Pine Streets

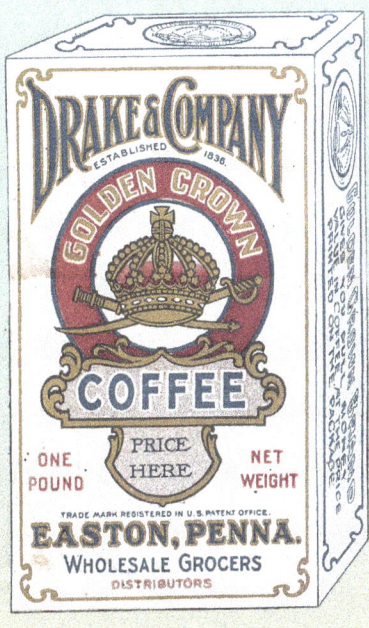

FURNITURE WAREROOMS & FACTORIES
OF
A. D. COOKE
SUCCESSOR TO
E. B. HOPKINS & DAVID GARIS
NOS 102 & 104
South 3rd St.
EASTON PA.
EST. 1848
WIDTH OF REAR 130 FEET.
DEPTH OF BUILDINGS 150 FEET.
HEIGHT OF STORE 60 FEET.
HEIGHT OF FACTORIES 40 FEET.
ENGINE 40 HORSE POWER
FULL WORKING CAPACITY 100 MEN.

NO MORE ROUND SHOULDERS.
—WEAR THE—
Knickerbocker SHOULDER Brace!
AND WALK UPRIGHT IN LIFE.
MANUFACTURED BY THE
Knickerbocker Brace Co.,
PRICES—75 cts., $1 and $1.50 per Pair.
N. A. JOHNSON, PROPRIETOR.
333 CHURCH STREET, EASTON, PENNA.

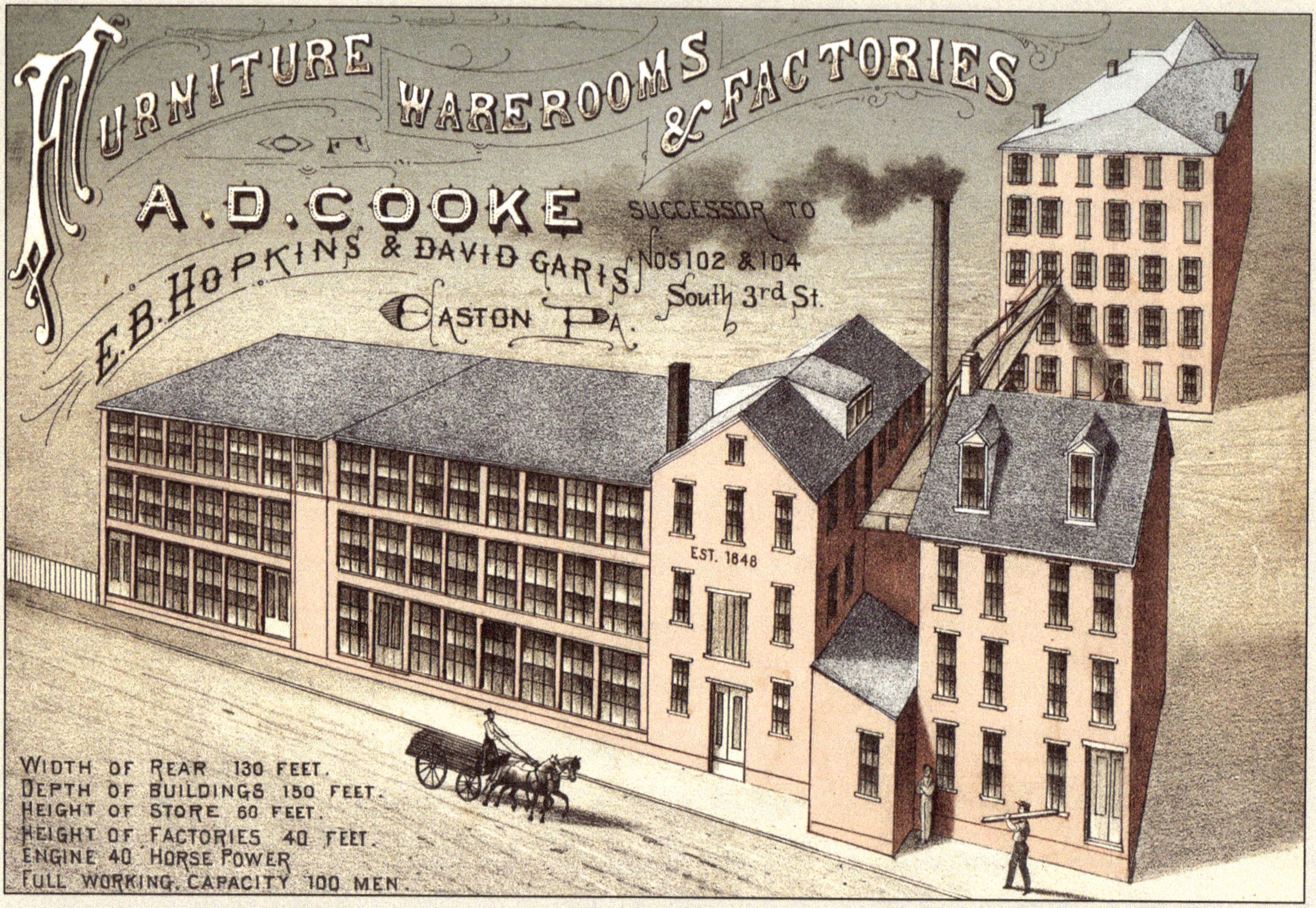

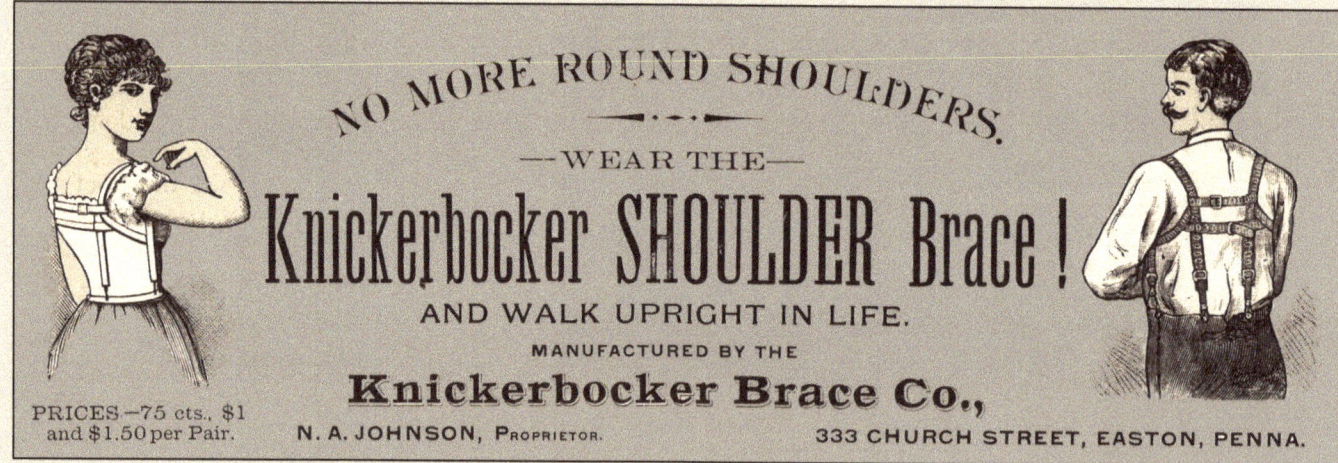

THE WALTER PURIFYING COMPANY

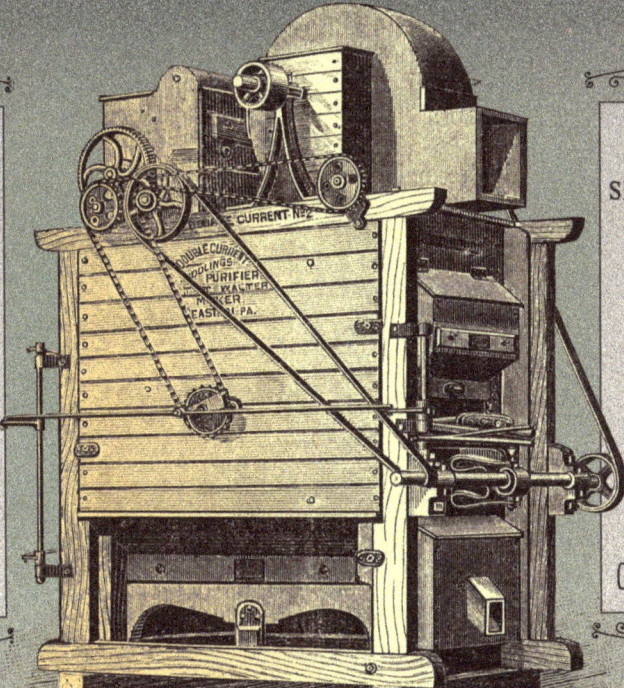

OUR SPECIALTIES.

Double Current Middlings PURIFIER, with Improved Balance Eccentric.

Walter's Elevating Centrifugal Reel.

Walter's Wheat Scouring Machines.

Walter's Wheat Separating Machines.

Walter's Aspirators.

Walter's Scalping Reels.

Walter's BRAN DUSTER, Elevator Heads and Feet, &c., &c.

DEALERS IN

SHAFTING,

PULLEYS,

HANGERS,

ROLLER MILLS,

BELTING,

ELEVATOR CUPS,

BOLTING CLOTHS,

&c., &c., &c.

CROWN SILK A SPECIALTY.

MANUFACTURERS OF
FLOUR MILL MACHINERY
-◎- EASTON, PA. -◎-

THE RESIDENCE OF HENRY GREEN IN 1877

City Hall in 1908

Southwest Corner of Third and Washington Streets

The Flood of 1903 at the Third Street Bridge

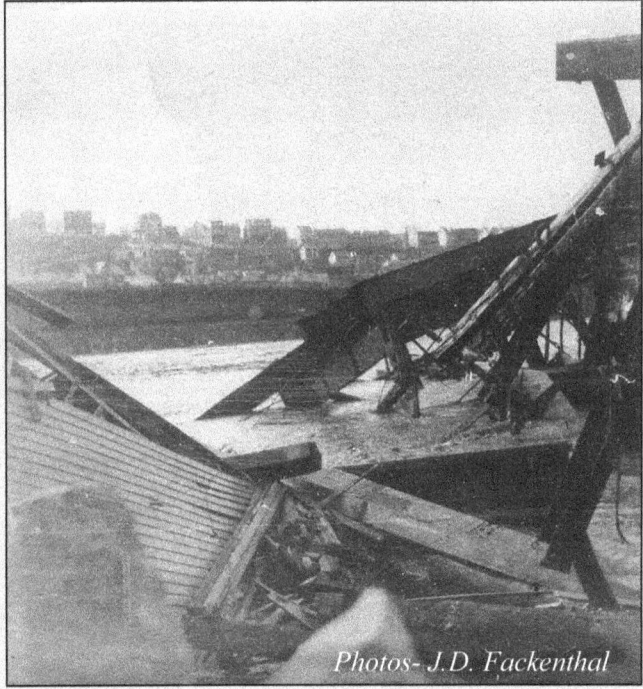

Photos- J.D. Fackenthal

Lehigh River Waterfront as seen from Mt. Ida

The Lehigh River at Easton served as one of the nation's earliest industrial centers. The Lehigh Canal, operated by the Lehigh Coal and Navigation Company, was completed as early as 1829. This canal primarily exported coal from Mauch Chunk to Easton, and then on to either the Delaware Canal or the Morris Canal (both completed in 1832). The Delaware Canal went from Easton to Bristol, Pennsylvania. The Morris Canal spanned from Phillipsburg to Paterson, New Jersey. This canal network put Easton at the juncture of trade that serviced the Philadelphia and New York City markets.

Looking Up the Lehigh River

When the railroads replaced the canals, the tracks were placed along some of the same routes as the canals to service the existing industries that were located along the Lehigh River. The Lehigh Valley Railroad is on the left, and the New Jersey Central Railroad is on the right. In the center, the Lehigh Canal, lockhouse, and canal boat can be seen, illustrating the payload difference that ultimately put an end to the canals.

Lehigh Valley Railroad Station on South Side behind Mt. Ida

Mount Ida

Mount Ida Coca-Cola Painting and Billboards

The Ingersoll-Sergeant Works along the Lehigh River in West Easton

Scandinavian inventor Simon Ingersoll created a steam-powered rock drill that he patented in 1871, and in 1874 the Ingersoll Rock Drill Company was established. In 1894, the company merged with the Seargent Drill Company and moved the new company from Manhattan to Easton. The Ingersoll-Sergeant works was built on land purchased from the Odenweller family in West Easton. This region was once known as Odenweller town. The company manufactured rock-drilling equipment. In 1903, the company opened another factory in Phillipsburg, New Jersey. By 1905, Ingersoll-Sergeant merged with Rand Drill Company to become Ingersoll Rand.

Simon Ingersoll

The Suspension Bridge Spanning the Lehigh River

Upper Suspension Bridge and Lehigh River, Easton, Pa.

A suspension bridge was built in 1886 that crossed the Lehigh River and connected the West Ward with the South Side of Easton. Many industries, such as the Railroad Yard pictured here, employed people who would commute by foot across the river. The walking bridge was damaged by wind in 1939 and rebuilt in 1940. A decade later, in 1950, the bridge was destroyed again by another wind storm. After more than six decades of service, the suspended walking bridge was demolished in 1951.

LEHIGH RIVER WATERFRONT AS SEEN FROM MT. IDA

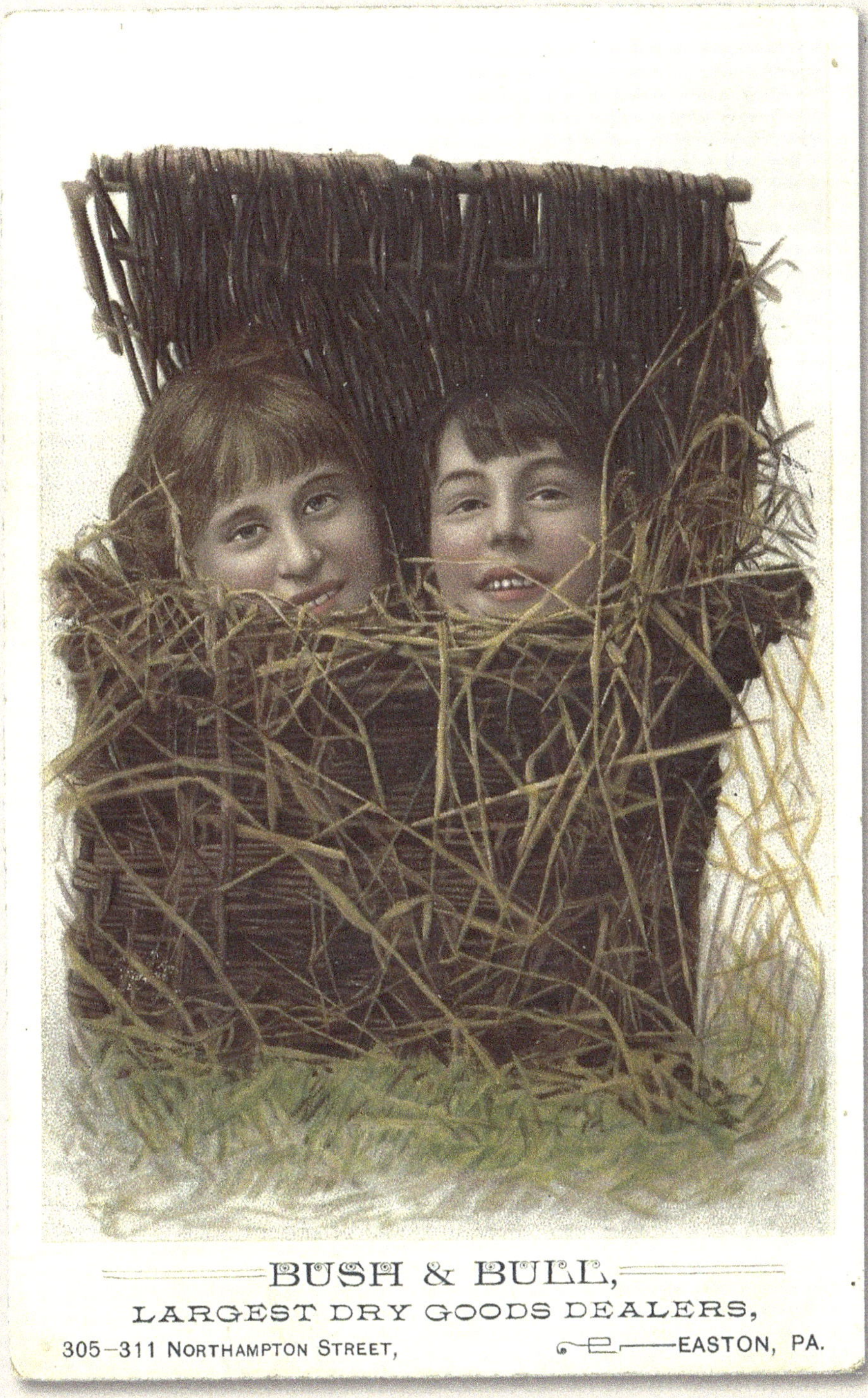
BUSH & BULL,
LARGEST DRY GOODS DEALERS,
305–311 NORTHAMPTON STREET, EASTON, PA.

WM. J. DAUB,
Manufacturer
Fine Furniture,
403 & 405 Northampton St.,
EASTON, PA.
Parlor & Chamber Suits a Specialty.

W. J. DAUB,
Furniture and Upholstering,
403 & 405 Northampton St.,
EASTON, PA.

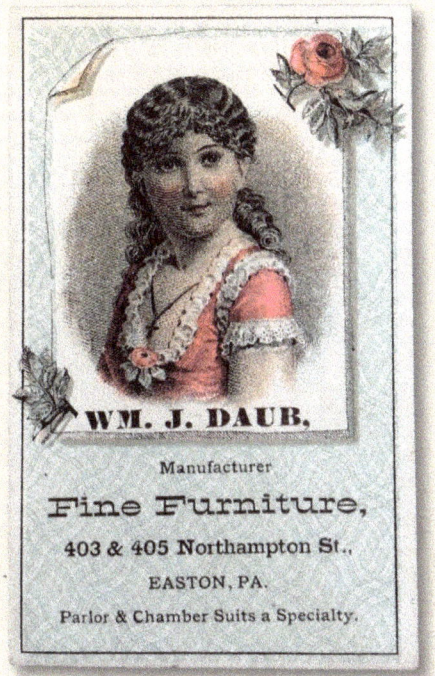

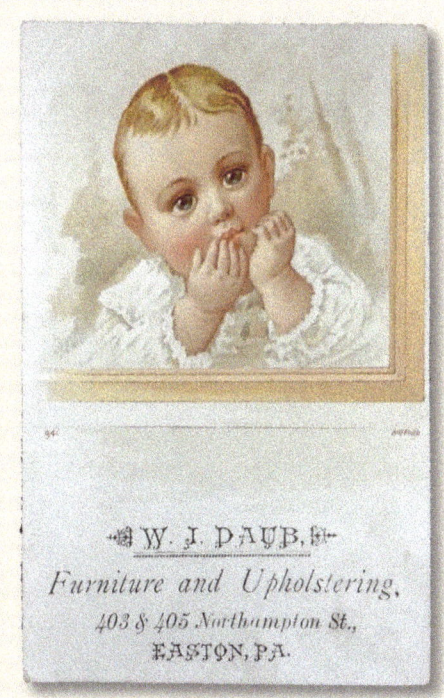

PARDEE HALL AT LAFAYETTE COLLEGE

Lafayette College

On December 27, 1824, a group of civic-minded citizens met at White's Hotel in Easton, where they resolved to establish a learning institution in the city of Easton. The name Lafayette College was chosen to honor the talents, virtues, and service of the great General Marquis de Lafayette in the cause of freedom. State legislation opposed and delayed the granting of the charter until March 9, 1826. Further complications regarding finding a president willing to base his salary and the faculty's salaries on tuition fees yet to be proven caused another delay, taking six more years to bring the institution into full fruition. On May 9, 1832, Lafayette College opened its doors in a rented farmhouse along the south banks of the Lehigh River. In attendance were 43 students and two professors. In 1834, nine acres were purchased, and the campus was moved to Mount Lafayette, the area now known as College Hill. Today, Lafayette College owns 20 percent of College Hill.

The Pardee Hall Fire of 1897

Pardee Hall was built in 1873. In 1879, the building was accidently destroyed by fire. After restoration, Pardee Hall was rededicated in 1880. On a December morning at 5 a.m. in 1897, a college janitor spotted a fire on the second floor in the west wing. He ran to the College Hill Fire Station to report the fire. When the College Hill firefighters arrived, they were unable to contain the fire. Blame for the lost firefight ranged from low water pressure, to lack of security, intoxicated firemen, and improper hoses. Investigators suspected arson. In June, a suspect was caught. George Herbert Stephens ironically had been an instructor in moral philosophy and ethics at Lafayette College from 1893 to 1897, and his contract had not been renewed. He served nine years in prison.

The Observatory at Lafayette College

Lafayette College

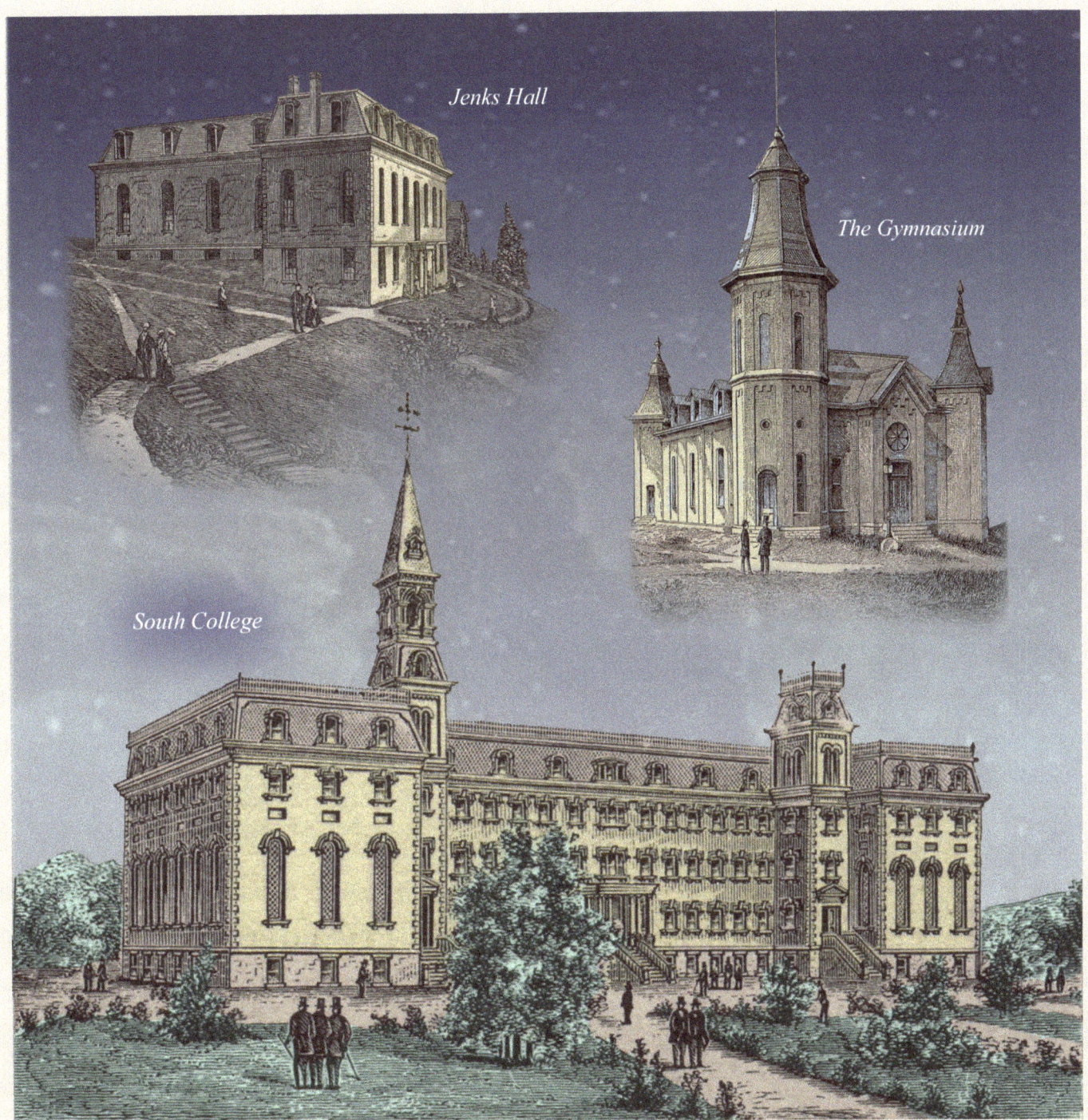

The Explosion of the Alfred Thomas as seen from New Jersey

On March 6, 1860, tragedy struck at Getter's Island on the Delaware River. The steamboat Alfred Thomas exploded on her maiden voyage. Built at the Easton boatworks, the Alfred Thomas was a flat bottom boat that was 87 feet long and 15 feet wide. The two 15 horsepower steam engines powered the stern paddle wheel, providing maximum power for the trip from Easton to Belvidere, New Jersey. The boat's builder, Thomas Bishop, had serious doubts concerning the installation of the boiler by the chief engineer, Sam Schaeff. These concerns were so serious that Bishop refused to get on board the boat he had just built. At 1:17 p.m., a loud blast was heard throughout the river valley. The boiler exploded, showering the area with boat and body parts. Passenger Eugene Troxel was blown 40 feet in the air and survived without a scratch. Twelve people were killed.

Z. TAYLOR

Fine Display of FANCY ROCKERS

FULL LINE OF Parlor and Chamber Suites.

FULL LINE OF Furniture and Bargains.

PERSONAL ATTENTION PAID TO THE UNDERTAKING BRANCH.

Established 1843.   Almost One-Half Century of Existence.

524 Northampton St. Easton, Pa.

THE PARSONS / TAYLOR HOME AT THE FOURTH AND FERRY STREETS

This home, built in 1757 by William Parsons, Surveyer General of Pennsylvania, also served as the home of George Taylor, signer of the Declaration of Independence.

Christ Lutheran Church at 4th and Ferry Streets

ROSENBAUM'S
Millinery Palace

☞ The Largest Establishment dealing EXCLUSIVELY in Millinery, in the Lehigh Valley.

THE LARGEST ASSORTMENT OF

Ladies', Misses' and Children's

TRIMMED AND UNTRIMMED

HATS AND BONNETS,

FLOWERS, FEATHERS, RIBBONS,

And Everything Pertaining To Millinery.

Nos. 407 & 409 Northampton Street, EASTON, PA.

Able's Opera House

Able's Opera House / Jewel Theater / Embassy Theater

Edward Able began construction of the Able Opera House in 1872. Located at 342 Northampton Street, the opera house featured performances by famous stars, such as Ethel and John Barrymore, E. L. Davenport, and Jenny Lind. In 1897, silent movies came into play, and the opera house featured "Projectoscopes" (silent movies scored by a live orchestra). By 1907, "The Jewel" nickelodeon theater was added. The Jewel Theater offered vaudeville shows and early talking movies. It was the largest theater in the area, featuring 1,000 seats. Two fires destroyed the theater, in 1924 and 1926, and it was reopened and expanded to 1,400 seats in 1927 and renamed the Embassy Theater. In 1957, the building was purchased by Arthur Sigal and converted to retail space. The Northampton County Historical and Genealogical Society purchased the property in 2003, and today the building houses the Sigal Museum that features and displays the history of Northampton County.

* Photos courtesy of Northampton County Historical and Genealogical Society

The Orpheum Theater on Front Street

The Seville / Boyd Theater on North Third Street

Designed in the Spanish atmospheric style, the Seville Theater was opened on February 21, 1929. The theater featured vaudeville acts and movies. In 1933, the Seville was purchased by Alexander Boyd of Philadelphia and renamed the Boyd Theater. The theater was purchased by businessmen who wanted to raze it for parking in 1971. More than 1,500 people signed a petition attempting to save it. In 1972, the Boyd Theater and the fight to save it were lost.

The Neumeyer Theatre

This granite facade was built in 1873 as the face of the Northampton National Bank. In 1910, the building was converted into the Neumeyer Theatre. The Neumeyer featured live vaudeville performances and silent movies. Between 1914 and 1916, the theater operated under the names of the Northampton and Colonial Theatres. During the vaudeville era, Easton played a role in debuting many of vaudeville's top stars and performances of the day.

In 1925, architect William H. Lee of Philadelphia was hired to expand and design a new theater, inspired by Spanish and Italian architecture. By 1926, the new theater opened as the State Theatre. Today the State is Easton's last remaining theater.

Photo courtesy of State Theatre Center for the Arts

The Prohibition Years

During the nineteen teens and the roaring twenties, Easton was known as somewhat of a party town. It was a city where the oldest hospitality profession flourished. Speakeasies and brothels prospered as elected leaders and law enforcement looked the other way. In 1915, Easton had 27 brothels. By the 1920s, there were 64 known brothels throughout Easton and surrounding townships. The 500 block of Pine Street was notorious for being the center of the prostitution trade. Moetta Newhart ran a brothel at 514-516 Pine Street. She was one of Easton's wealthiest and most famous residents. As prohibition locked down the nation's bar rooms, Easton's speakeasies continued to do business. While the Bushkill, Kuebler, and Seitz breweries were forced to shut down, orginized crime moved in. Many neighbors of the Seitz Brewery were paid off in beer and hush money to stay quiet and keep watch. If beer was being pumped out onto Bushkill Street, that was a sign that a federal raid was about to happen. Local law enforcement was also on the payroll. When two federal officers failed to prove their identification during a raid at the Seitz Brewery, local police had them detained as "imposters" while evidence was removed from the brewery. After Prohibition was lifted, Easton lost its monopoly on speakeasies, and the local breweries struggled to compete with the larger national brands during the Great Depression. In 1932, Herbert F. Laub became the Northampton County district attorney. Laub cracked down on the brothels that he claimed were connected to gangsters, gambling, and guns. In 1943, Moetta Newhart's Pine Street brothel closed when she was put on trial and sentenced to a year in prison.

Laubach's Department Store on the 300 block of Northampton Street

Easton High School

North Second Street Looking East

NORTHAMPTON STREET LOOKING WEST

NORTHAMPTON STREET LOOKING EAST

North Fourth Street Facing North

South Fourth Street Facing South

North Third Street Facing North

South Third Street Facing South

South Third Street Facing North

The Farmers Market at Center Square

Northampton Street Facing East from Center Square

Center Square Facing Southeast

The Abandoned Dixie Plant

As the sun set on the manufacturing era in the northeast, Easton had been challenged with what the non-industrial definition of Easton would be. Suburban sprawl, combined with declining industry, presented Easton with many challenges for decades. Sadly, the empty promise of the Urban Renewal programs of the 1960s and 1970s left Easton with a large portion of its historic architecture destroyed. Communities were displaced, and for a while, Easton was not getting the respect and attention that it deserved. Through the efforts of many individuals, over several decades, the groundwork for revival was laid. Many neglected and abandoned buildings were restored. The historic preservation movement inspired restorations and helped bring Easton back into a positive light. Recent years have brought a shift in demographics and a national interest in walkable communities. The cultural limitations of suburbia have left some people looking for more community interaction and a return to urban living. Easton has started yet another chapter in its long history. This new chapter defines Easton as an arts community, restaurant hub, festival destination, and interesting place to live. As development returns to Easton, it is important to realize that history is one of our primary assets. Architectural preservation is critical in keeping Easton's unique aesthetic. Development can complement or compromise the historic beauty that defines Easton. The confluence of the Lehigh and Delaware Rivers has attracted people to this region for centuries. As we enter the next phase of Easton's future, let's embrace the spirt of Easton's colorful past.

PRESENT-DAY CENTER SQUARE FARMERS MARKET, HELD HERE SINCE 1752

Photo courtesy of Greater Easton Development Partnership

About the Cover

The Easton Gas and Electric Company gifted the city of Easton and the Easton Board of Trade this 2000-light sign in 1909. This sign was placed so that it could be seen by passengers traveling on the eight railroads that passed through Easton. Easton was the first American city to utilize the concept of an electric-lighted municiple sign to advertise the city. The concept was conceived by consultant George Williams of New York City to help recruit industry and increase the population of Easton in order to increase revenue for the electric company. The letters on the word "Easton" were 10 feet tall. A flickering image of a rising sun symbolized the dawning of a new day of opportunity. For many years the "Easton City of Resources" sign flashed its message from dusk until midnight.

A second illuminated sign was also donated to the city of Phillipsburg, New Jersey, and hung on the other side of the river at Union Square Station in order to help orient train travelers.

About the Author

Photo by Adam Atkinson

Native Eastonian Bruce Fackenthal has had a preoccupation with Easton's past since childhood. His interest in Easton's history began as a young bottle-digger seeking out old bottles that came from Easton breweries. Bruce has been collecting Easton breweriana and memorabilia since the age of 12. Phillipsburg historian Ronald Wynkoop's book *Forks of the Delaware Area* was an early source of curiosity for Bruce, leading to a lifetime of uncovering Easton's past. Bruce's passion for historic preservation has resulted in purchasing and restoring award-winning historic buildings in downtown Easton. Bruce has spent his professional life as a graphic designer, illustrator, art director, art educator, and historic preservationist. Bruce's design background and passion for Easton's history have come togther as the perfect combination to create *Easton: City of Resources*.

CENTER SQUARE IN 1910

References

The Alfred Thomas Explosion - www.wfmz.com June 10, 2011
Able's Opera House - https://sigalmuseum.org/locations/sigal-museum
Binney and Smith - Crayola Corporate Communications
City of Resources Sign - *Technical World Magazine* 1911
Dixie Cup Factory - https://sites.lafayette.edu/dixiecollection/scope-content-note
Easton during Prohibition - Lehighvalleylive June 21, 2018| by Rudy Miller
Karldon Hotel - *Morning Call* December 24, 1998| by S.M. Parkhill
Kuebler Brewery - *American Breweriana Journal* July/August 2014 By Rich Wagner /*American Journal of Progress* 1876
Lafayette College - *Morning Call* 2020 8/7 S. M. Parkhill / Lafayette Centennial Publication 1932
Neumeyer Theatre - www.statetheatre.org
Paxinosa Inn Trolley - *Morning Call* 1997 11/18 S. M. Parkhill
The Philadelphia and Easton Electric Railway - *The Intelligencer* March 27, 2016| by Edward Levinson
Howard Rinek - *Morning Call* December 30, 1997| by S.M. Parkhill
Seitz Brewery - *American Breweriana Journal* July/August 2014 By Rich Wagner
Seville/Boyd Theater - www.cinematreasures.org
Herman Simon - en.wikipedia.com/www.wfmz.com History's Headlines November 4, 2014

From the oldest known painting of Easton. Courtesy Howard P. Kinsey

EASTON IN 1810

Acknowledgements

I would like to thank and recognize the people who shaped my passion for local history and helped me better understand the achievements of the people who came before us, and how different, and yet familiar Easton must have been in the past.

Leonard Buscemi
Rev. Uzal W. Condit
Mike Fackenthal
Forks of the Delaware Bottle Collectors Association
Richard Hope
James Lee
William J. Heller
A.D. Chidsey, Jr
Illustrators - S. Kind, Tinky, Rookhout
Jim Wright
Ron Wynkoop
Photographers and postcard retouchers of yesteryear

Special thanks for production assistance:

Jennifer Bright (Proofing/Publishing)
Catherine Fackenthal (Proofing)
Frank Mitman (color proofing)

www.ingramcontent.com/pod-product-compliance
Lightning Source LLC
Chambersburg PA
CBHW051357110526
44592CB00023B/2865